The Limitless Heart

The Limitless Heart: New and Selected Poems
(1997–2022)

Cheryl Boyce-Taylor

Haymarket Books
Chicago, Illinois

Published in 2023 by
Haymarket Books
P.O. Box 180165
Chicago, IL 60618
773-583-7884
www.haymarketbooks.org
info@haymarketbooks.org

ISBN: 978-1-64259-972-5

Distributed to the trade in the US through Consortium Book
Sales and Distribution (www.cbsd.com) and internationally
through Ingram Publisher Services International (www.
ingramcontent.com).

This book was published the generous support of Lannan
Foundation, Wallace Action Fund, and the Marguerite Casey
Foundation.

Special discounts are available for bulk purchases by organizations
and institutions. Please email info@haymarketbooks.org for more
information.

Cover artwork by Kate Quarfordt.
Cover design by Rachel Cohen.

Library of Congress Cataloging-in-Publication data is available.

Entered into digital printing August 2023

For Ceni

For Boyce Blackette,
my twin brother, 1950

And for
Mariahadessa Ekere Tallie
& Ntozake Shange

Contents

The Limitless Heart

Acknowledgments

Foreword

Surrender to self, to the seasons, to the moon, to the more
or less long day. Fruit harvest. And always and everywhere in
the slightest manifestations, the primacy of the plant, the plant trampled
underfoot but still alive, dead but reviving, the plant free. . .
    —Suzanne Césaire, "Malaise d'une civilisation," *Tropiques #5*, April
1942. Translated by Keith L. Walker (*The Great Camouflage*, 2012).

Cheryl Boyce-Taylor's *The Limitless Heart* is a momentous record of the poet's
work across nearly four decades and six previously published books, in-
cluding *Mama Phife Represents,* which chronicles the years following the death
of her dearly beloved son, Malik "Phife Dawg" Taylor, of the legendary A
Tribe Called Quest. Beginning with poems written in the mid-1980s and
culminating with new poems written during lockdown—between 2020
and 2022—*The Limitless Heart* is the lifework of a Black, lesbian poet and cul-
tural worker steeped in Black feminist practices—mothered and mothering
in the whirlwind.

    Cheryl Boyce-Taylor was born in Arima, Trinidad on December 6,
1950. As she writes it in "Black":

she be a Black woman
born between a town's whisper
and a slither moon

she be Ibeji woman
born in hard crop guava season
between calabash and casava
she be the dust of Arima mountains

Here is a poet who understands herself in relation to the earth,
the seasons, the dust, moon, and mountains, and the people shaped by
these elements. "[B]orn Ibeji," the twin of a brother who died in utero,
Boyce-Taylor is in deep communication with those who have passed out

of life and into new material. In this way, I think of hers as a poetics of relationship. This informs some of what her poems are reaching toward, as well as the political commitments she articulates across her life, from her own politicization as a young person on a trip to Huntsville, Alabama ("they killed Martin Luther King Jr. my life changed / Amerika devoured whatever bloomed light I grew inside") to the work of creating cultural spaces of kinship and restoration *inside the belly* of patriarchal, white supremacist regimes in the United States.

These political commitments cannot be separated from the spiritual centers of her work. In an interview with the writer, Caits Meissner, for PEN America in 2022, Meissner suggests that Boyce-Taylor's poems are altars. Boyce-Taylor responds, "The naming of objects helps me to stay grounded in my Trinidadian roots, the use of dialect keeps my grandmother's voice attached to the red Arima dust of my birth. I am always a part of my land that holds my twin brother's naval string." And then later: "I knew when I grew up I wanted to work in the service of story, memory, and community. Each poem is a prayer, each poem is an ancestral altar, a promise to the land, a vision I want to always hold, and never lose." This poet, so utterly rooted to the vegetal and spiritual possibilities of place, holds memory and language as central to an emancipatory practice:

> "comewhispermycomrades/ripmyachelikesadstorms/untiltheylaydownmy body / until they lay down my pen" and "i knelt to catch the crooked water / falling from her mouth   testify // what are the names of our sons . . ."

Boyce-Taylor was raised under the loving, protective eye of her mother, Elma, who recited poems and worked as a nursery school teacher, first aid instructor, math tutor, milliner, and swim instructor in their town. The poet remembers: "She actually put me on her back when we went on family outings to the river, it was generally a common practice for her to treat little girls in our family that way. On more than one occasion I fell asleep on her back[,] this is all true." Out of these memories—saturated with family and closeness—emerges a portrait of a profound love between mother and daughter, but also Boyce-Taylor's childhood with the river, plants, and her people.

As she recalls, Boyce-Taylor shared a bed with her mother from birth until she left Trinidad for New York City at the age of thirteen. In an interview with the writer and scholar, Ana-Maurine Lara in 2007, Boyce-Taylor notes: "Well, I guess the biggest thing in my life, and it still remains that, was when I was thirteen years old I left Trinidad, my home and everything I knew, including my mother and father, to travel to New York to live with my mother's sister. In St. Albans, Queens. [...] I felt like I would die, almost. And it was during that time that I began writing lots of letters asking for me to come back home to Trinidad. But, the plan was already in place that my brother and she would join me here."

This departure is a defining cleaving which runs through all of her work. As such, she begins this selected works with "Yearning." For those who read the book from front to back, yearning for home becomes the tunnel through which we access all else:

ah yearning
for voices ringing shrill
from B-flat to high-C
bamsee rolling
one hand on left hip
de other flying
leaping in meh face

oh gosh ah yearning
yearning   Yeeeeeeeeeearning
hungry for meh people.

Hers is a cry made of being rooted in a place and then being pulled from it. This leaving shapes her mouth and sound. But hers is also a cry of finding a route—in imagination and language—to that homeplace again.

In the same interview with Ana-Maurine Lara, Boyce-Taylor tells the story of an assignment her teacher gave her when she was eight years old.

The teacher said she wanted her to travel and to write about those travels before coming back to school in September. Boyce-Taylor remembers: "Looking back, she did not literally mean get on an airplane and travel. She meant, travel in fantasy. And somehow I knew that. I don't know how I knew that, but I knew it. And so I wrote about all these places I visited and traveled. And I wrote a bunch of essays and I think that I loved the fantasy of it. And that was when it got in my blood."

I think about how this teacher was instructing her to imagine, to fly, to travel in mind. I think about how she speaks of her father, "encouraging [her] to speak honestly—bold and boisterous. A rarity for a Caribbean dad" in the 1950s. I think of the poet's mother reciting verses to her children, such as Alfred Tennyson's "Cannon to right of them, / Cannon to left of them, / Cannon behind them / Volleyed and thundered. . .". I think of these sounds, the sounds of her life—a woman chanting in the market, birds in Arima trees, the voice of her brilliant son coming into his own immense sound. I think of this poet's grandmother picking her medicine from the garden before rushing off to attend the births. I think of this poet whose twin died in utero. I think of how she is also the mother of twins, one who died and one who lived, "one would hear river talking / the other would write it down / one would change the world / the other would leave it..." I think of this poet practicing social work in New York City in the 1980s, going to theater practice, raising a child, being married to a husband, and then following her sexuality out of that marriage, her "coming out" as lesbian. I think of this poet studying with Audre Lorde who asked, "What would happen if you wrote the things you really wanted to say? Who is holding a gun to your head and preventing you from saying the things you must say?" and how Cheryl says ". . . I began to sob. I knew that I was the one holding the gun to my own head." I think of what it must have taken for this poet to metabolize this moment into a poetics of radiant, radical truth—in touch with her whole self, as in "my mouth eh ha no cover / me eh fraid nobody yu know . . . ".

I think of this poet, raised by mothers who cooked in the yard and took, in their hands, the good, green leaves of Wonder-of-the-World. How out of the vibrant root-energies of her life, motherhood, and lineage, this poet's languages emerge, flourishing with azaleas, hibiscuses, marigolds. In this way, these poems are polyvocal, polytemporal *places* full of plant medicine, record, warning, and a path into a dense forest, a sovereign world of reunions inside of this one.

Boyce-Taylor writes: "from wind's beak once fell two seeds / one a bird the other a girl / turned wild sorrel tree." What follows are the words only this wild sorrel could make.

aracelis girmay
Brooklyn, New York, 2022

Introduction

The Limitless Heart: New and Selected Poems (1997–2022) is a collection that represents seven books and thirty years of writing. In this collection, I've written about migration, Type I Diabetes, women's rights, racism, discrimination, love, poverty, and Black lives that matter. I share my experiences of being a daughter, mother, and wife, and of living as a queer woman. Each collection is in conversation with the book that preceded it. My stories hide very little, because I come from a family that kept many secrets and was not outwardly affectionate. Despite that, we children knew we were loved by the daily sacrifices our parents made to keep us clothed, fed, and educated. In our tiny Caribbean island of Trinidad, an education was the most prized possession a parent could give a child.

As a young girl, I listened as my mom sang, memorized, and recited long poems around our home. She loved poetry, and passed this life-saving gift on to me. I've taken the privilege and challenge to remember, as best I can, my childhood journey from Victory Street, Arima, to St. Albans, Queens, and finally my arrival as an adult poet woman in my beloved Clinton Hill, Brooklyn. Over the years, some of my writing has been a bit hurtful for my family. They have accused me of telling family secrets in my poems, making them feel exposed. After my grandmother's death, I realized that her family secrets were also mine to tell. Secrets can keep a woman from maturing and expanding. Healing and growth can only take place when secret wounds are uncovered and allowed to breathe. Poems have sustained me since I was a little girl.

Losing my son, Malik, was as painful as leaving my home and all the family I ever knew in Trinidad. I was thirteen when my mother sent me to New York City to live with her sister, who I did not know very well. My aunt was helpful, providing shelter and education, but she was not prepared to offer affection or mothering, having not had much mothering herself. She was the older sister to eleven siblings. Yet she worked hard, provided, and shared my love of poetry.

While I had been exposed to poems all of my life, poetry became truly mine in the third grade when as a part of our weekly curriculum we recited poems by heart under the tall breezy trees every Tuesday afternoon. I can still feel the words floating in that sweet breeze all around my head. At the end of that year, when we went on summer break, my favorite teacher, Miss Charles, told the class that while we were enjoying our time off visiting friends and traveling with our families, we should write poems, letters, and stories to document how we spent our summer vacation. You will each share it with the class when you return in September, Miss Charles told us. It would be years before I understood her strategy. She knew our families did not have money for travel, but she wanted to plant a seed of fantasy and adventure in us. I was intrigued and ran with the assignment. I have been running with it ever since!

Once I was in NYC, I missed my mom greatly. Outside of crying almost every day, the only thing that gave me comfort was reading poems and writing letters to her. As I grew into young adulthood, I sought joy and solace in poetry. Then I began writing in dialect to keep close to my family's language and culture; it reminds me of a place and people with whom I once felt happy, safe, and protected. I started attending readings to be in the world of poets of the Black Arts Movement. I was a new mom when I discovered the poet Nikki Giovanni. She was reading at Queens College, and I took my baby with me to hear her read. She wowed me! Her poems were about resistance, Black power, Black pride, women's rights, self-love, and Black love. She declared that we came from a mighty history that we must be proud of. Nikki Giovanni read with such power and female authority that I knew that public poetry was something I could do well. I became obsessed with the music of Gil Scott-Heron and The Last Poets. I began writing political poems and adored the work of African-American poets like June Jordan, Amiri Baraka, and later, Ntozake Shange, Cheryl Clarke, Sonia Sanchez, and Sekou Sundiata. As much as I loved them, I kept looking for myself in their work. I just knew that one day I would turn a page and smell mangoes, curry chicken, roast breadfruit, and callaloo.

Where was the girl with that loud and rowdy dialect, calypso and backwater stories in patois written all over her? It was not until I found Derek Walcott and read Dionne Brand's *No Language Is Neutral* that I found my sweet spot. Dionne's work spoke of political unrest in Grenada, Trinidad, and other Caribbean islands. She spoke about the daub of black shine sea on bush smoke land, the pulse of heart stretching up to Maracas Bay. She spoke about ocean and wind, about walking the rocks and listening to the silence of the water. She spoke about lesbian love. . . and then I was in my element.

For almost forty years I have been working towards creating and sustaining a Caribbean poetry movement in the US. In 1994, I was the first Caribbean Woman to perform my poetry in Trinidadian dialect at the National Poetry Slams in Asheville, North Carolina. I was one of four poets that represented New York City on the Nuyorican Poetry Slam team. We were joyous when we placed third out of about twenty other teams. Later that year I established the Calypso Muse Reading Series. My goal was to produce the works of Caribbean poets reading and writing in dialect. It was a huge success. Beyond the readings, I offered workshops, retreats, and scholarships, published anthologies, and hosted book release parties. Over the years I realized that the work of Caribbean writers began to go fall off, and there were not many opportunities for their new and published works. I'm presenting these new and selected poems now because in the current climate we are living in we cannot slow down. It is more important than ever to record our family stories so that our voices and our history are not lost. I would not dream of letting this moment pass me by and for that reason, I add my voice and my work as a Caribbean woman writer to the Caribbean canon. I am following in the footsteps of Lillian Allen, Kwame Dawes, Derek Walcott, Dionne Brand, Claudia Rankine, Linton Kwesi Johnson, Jean Binta Breeze, Lorna Goodison, Kamau Braithwaite, and Michelle Cliff to name a few. It is with great love and gratitude that I offer *The Limitless Heart*. I am hoping that you too will allow your heart to be limitless.

In my writing, I walk with honesty, trying to always remember and apply what my ancestors told me. This is my open door, my limitless heart.

3

Come in. Dream, laugh, and cry with me. In this collection, I have shared the things that burn the brightest in me. As Audre Lorde once told me, if you cannot find what you want to see in the world, write it yourself.

Cheryl Boyce-Taylor
New York City, 2022

Raw Air

(1997)

YEARNING

A long white space
with blue dots and orange lines
a wide winter space

for hummingbird sounds
steel pan pounds
a space turned out
with yearning

ay say ah yearning
ah say   ah have   ah yearning
ah yeeeeeeearning   yearning
for nite tepid breeze
big fat moon dat eh fraid   yuh
big moon shining
like meh neighbor Merle face

oh god ah yearning
for mango doudouce
sticky and sweeeeet
for melongen   curry cabbage
and blue dasheen

ah yearning
to see de green jaundiced eyes
of Ratty mangy dog smiling
after he eat up de saltfish bone
de chiney man throw for he

ah yearning for—
"gurl come out de canal
ah go tell yuh mudder
yuh cursing"

ah yearning for—

"oman whey meh kiss-meh-ass food
oui pappa it sounding
like yuh vex"

"oh god ease meh up
nah darling
yuh can't see ah nursing
de baby"

"buwha de ass wrong wid dis oman
she tink ai iz a hen"
"use de stove broda"

ah yearning
for meh ole goat Sheela
de textile gate up Victory Street
where ah let she drop she shit balls
one at a time
in de white people yard

ah yearning
for stan'pipe water
an belly full breadfruit
chennet to make meh tongue tight
an mauby so ah could pee bitter

ah yearning
yearning for she got me hot
an ah cuss she ass
ah call she mudder ah prostitute
my mouth eh ha no cover
me eh fraid nobody yuh know

ah yearning to drag tongue
up Fredrick Street an
mass oh mass in meh ass

ah yearning for rum shop
Christmas parang
and obeah to get de man ah want
ah lil blue bag to swell de foot
ah he chile mudder belly

ah yearning for roti and
roast corn by Curepe Junction
a nice cold Carib
to send it down

ah yearning
for voices ringing shrill
from B-flat to high-C
bamsee rolling
one hand on left hip
de other flying
leaping in meh face

o gosh ah yearning
yearning   Yeeeeeeeeearning
hungry for meh people.

Forever Arima

Tanty Girlie's poem

my Arima mountains closer
my dead twin weaves a pink hibiscus
bouquet for my ankles   welcomes me back
to the house of our birth
a faint steelpan punctuates this calypso
night

ai gurl long time ai eh see yuh
yuh doh come here for love nor for money
ten years yuh away   sombody do yuh sometin
I am aroused by the lilt
of my peoples voices

the kitchen shelves no longer house
temptations of my childhood
guava jelly   tamarind jam   coconut drops
all replaced by see-thru bottles of curry, jerk
sauce
processed pepper imported from Caracas

the yellow and gold plastic fly cover
keeps the sweet bread insect-free
nothing protects me as the memories come
hard and sweet fragile and scathing

but wait nah, wha yuh mudder, my sister
sayin bout dat dread lock ting on yuh head?
she please? . . . ok, me too.

Tantan Rose begins at dawn
gathering provision
yamatoota   tanya   dasheen
sits me down to say. . . -ting change gurl

here com bad jus like america

        heat oil in skillet
        1/4 cup sugar
1/2 cup chopped garlic

de young people laazzy
doh want to work hard
cussin de parents
well ai never

        4 cups rice
        1 cup chopped pig tails

drugs wash away dis place
de neighbor boy, Ms. Martil
'bout sixteen years so on "coke"
you remember he?
he iz de one break in de
ole lady house
lord . . . hit she in she head
oh meh lord gawd

        bowl of spinach
        bowl of okra

take she Sunday school
change eat she sweet bread
hit she in she head
she nearly dead

        dash of salt   paprika

yu remember Marcia
six chiren still no husband
makin' de poor mudder shame

2 cups pigeon peas
8 cracked blue crabs

de biggest sister pass
O levels yes . . . workin'
in de Red House   Red House . . .
is like de white house over there
yeh man Red House

1/4 cup bird pepper

de boro lay off de fader and half
de older workmen
shame shame, eh?

1/4 cup old oak rum

oh shrimps look at de time
yuh want som bread an shark
while yuh waitin
food nearly finish we gurl

dash some hot pepper on
sip som rum
stir de callaloo
lil curry lil pepper

chile raisin' chiren now eh easy nah
lordy   lordy   gimme a lil rum
ai glad mine nearly grown

ah   thin   thin   sip ah   oak

still smooth gurl—

add lil water tu rice

brown de chicken
sip som rum

so yuh com tu see meh
or tu play mas tell de trut
ten days eh no vacation
yuh really americanize yes gurl

mo pepper
lil bit oak

oh make sure yuh tek off dem
gold bracelets before yuh go out tonite eh
dey robbin' yuh in Maxi taxi
in broad daylite
ai tellin' yuh when de take in 2 rum
any number could play

      1/4 cup ground ginger
      sprig of mint
      a pinch of rum
      chinke lil bit mo

sweeten up yuh chops gurl
yuh doh eat so in america, eh?
Sunday food on Friday
de kitchen smellin' nice   nice
dinner go be good tonite . . .

      brown de chicken
      brown de chicken down
      sip som rum
      brown de chicken
      le we eat

grandma's rocker has the same old squeak
my twin comes close peeks in at me

in the distance Ma Subar fat cock crows
through the open door my aunt's voice

"-nite yes gurl,
but look at meh sister dauter nah
sleep well   til' mornin' eh."

MIST

Kisses you once placed
on my neck and arms
are now the compass i use
to chart your absence
blue ink traces mist
on the window
a faint reminder
that you were here

so often
i am caught breathless
a thin string dangling
in your perfume
like a dog sniffing trees
trying to find my way home.

LETTER TO LOVE

Oh love you sent in spring
this bright blue bird
with cobalt feathered brow
a radiant hand of flowers
dangling from thickening stems

how beautiful the wind
that blew my heart to bits
against her purple breast

oh love,
just as my sight was failing
and all the world seemed dulled
with pretense

just when i thought my flannel
sheets would be the last safe hands
to caress my naked body

she came with her two-color eyes
her dancing mane in shades of tinted brown
deep pleats of orange laughter
hiding in her blue-moon breast

oh love, at last i rose
to catch each shiny ray of moon
to conspire with the stars
about silver ribbons for her hair

one streak of copper sun
with amber beads i fastened
to her neck

her mouth rare colored murals
parted like the sea

and love, dear god
she was radiant

oh love you sent me
this amber-tinted girl
with undulating dances
like the wind

to shake my legs
and fill my arms
in that winter which grew so cold

from my window
in this new reign of spring
i see the red and purple dahlias
bloom again
these sobs that break this season
shakes my heart like new

oh love
oh love why didn't you
send me rain instead?

For My Comrades*

For Billy Fogarty

something's rumbling tonight
loud noises   a car firing off
a tire   an uzi   9 millimeter

and i want to take the crazy ass
#4 train outta here
bus   plane   amtrak   anything

something's jumping off
someone's jacking off
let me say there will be no more
riots no more move bombings
no more fucking bussing
no more mumia   no more biko

i will not sit at the back of the bus
will not keep my mouth shut
rage is essential
i carry it like the babies
i can no longer bare

you want my nappy head
and all i want is the music of wind
listen to my drum
i am trinidad's daughter
first offspring of shango

pass me a cup of ganja tea
and excuse me god dammit
i am tamarind woman
tempering earthquakes under my feet

i cut my hair in full moon

root it under banana bush
pin bullets to my petticoats
wear grenades in my shoes

rage is an aphrodisiac
i ride your fear
like an oversized cock

be afraid

this is a warning
i will not be silent
i will not sit at the back of the bus

there will be no more grenada
no more panama
no more tupac shakur

something is rumbling tonight

there will be no more apartheid
this is not the old south africa
i will not keep my mouth shut
i will not sit at the back of the bus

come whisper my comrades
rip my ache like sad storms
until they lay down my body
until they lay down my pen
whichever falls first

* conference on race 12/12/96 nyc

Night When Moon Follows

(2000)

NIGHT

when the ceiling
is cellophane

i rise find myself
at the center of the quarry

where my grandfather rode
his donkey every day

his face and hair yellow
as the sand pebbles he blast

into dust for cement
to build houses

my lime bedsheets the chariot
that has flown me here

a white pillow locked securely
around my head for flight

tonight i need no clothes
shoes no insulin needles

only this head of cowry adorned locks
a shawl that warms me

moon white as swiss cheese
angles herself transports me

my rigid disobedient spine
curves into a million branches

grandfather is afraid i tell his secrets
shallow stream that he is

mocks his own daughters
as he pounds their mother's flesh

he's teaching them to be afraid of sleep
afraid of love the looking glass

what they have learned about loneliness
wide as the crack in father's head

father breaks stepmother's arm
she cooks cleans for him cries for me

makes me promise never to marry
a man blind unable to see his mirror

in his own daughter's eyes

grandfather
the dead do not see
what looking glass have you left your daughters?

PIARCO

On de way to de airport near Arouca
cousin Chandra ask
which i like best
american summer nights
that stay bright bright way past eight o'clock
or thick Trini evenings
sky burstin black and white wid stars
an mosquito and sandfly
fightin fer yuh skin

i eh sayin notin
bu memory is ah bitch
when yuh melancholy
an leavin yuh family

ah only remembering de las ten days
tropical sun stirring hot in meh belly
like when yuh wid chile

de cousin chatting   chatting
only lil fine talk
ah hearin she bu ah quiet
she voice anxious   thick
thick as de July heat

she askin meh
how i like de nights i spend here
what i goin to tell auntie for she
if i think de curry will seep through
de bag an mess up de plane—

me i drifting
going to meh new home
thirty years later
an it still new

yuh sleepin
wha yuh tinkin so deep bout
cousin sayin   *chat*   *chat*
dis woman fraid if she silent

wha go happen

bu i goin home
a place meh mother could
never get used to callin dat   home
she could never get used to light
on in de house whole day
stupidness   pure stupidness

dese americans
is extravagant dey extravagant
in restaurant every night   huh
nomme   credit card hey wahizdat
wha iz dat

my father teach me long time
never owe nobody notin
and i don't . . .

i floatin loss in de sugarcane stalks
an de blue sinking clouds
kiss meh nah girl
cousin sayin

now de plane high   high
oh god sky fer so
shit man all ah de red hill gone
all de sea water
is only me now
and dis dark night
to hide dese tears

yes is me an me alone
an de zaboca tree
outside gramma bedroom window
eh even kno ah gone yet

WEEP

Father i've searched every line
of your unwritten letters
to encounter one clue
you and my mother together

that prized moment
did she cover her eyes did she laugh
cover her mouth in girlish shyness
did you cradle the spot
where her hairline begins

mother i've searched
every laugh line
every small shading
on back your neck
your root dark hands

to find a sign
any kind   how did you
how did you
did you love my father

i remember my father's
big feet identical to mine
i remember his hard back
the future bristling
yoked around bulging muscles
working up a sweat on his upper arms

how the years would take from it
render it limp and bleeding
how the alcohol would rub those
muscles   thin

rob our family of its dreams

the incorrigible pint of brew
turning and turning sour
in his girl's eyes
night after night she would
read poems and prayers

sing poems and prayers
night after night

embalming herself with holy ghost
marrying herself to god
her one bad leg pin cushioned
with secrets
limping with details of denial

mother did you weep
father did you   did you
and did you love my mother

so proud
she ironed play clothes
what lessons shall i learn
within the confines of this stiff collar
this stilled tongue

SKULL

For Malik

when for years i could not tell
could not chase away
skeletons from my closet
we ate cake drank beer smoked
marijuana joints

and God you must have wondered
how a Christian girl could
sin so low

despite the sugar rise
i must be normal
glucose levels break
high off charts
sugar out of control   *must be normal*
400   lost another baby

sugar rise   rise   345
380   counting losses
a tingling right arm
another baby   an eyesight
a toenail a breast on a plate

glucose up   up
control machine beeps
in my hand
could not see my boy
running to my arms
mommy mommy some sugar please

gimme somsuga'
his dad used to say
biting his toes his tummy

the boy would laugh
fall helpless on the bed
on his mommy

mommy suga'

sun falls brilliant on rough rocks
child falls into my arms
i wear his arms
like a cross
around my neck
clasp my boy's hands
a holy bible to my lips

are you watching God
can't pass this sweet venom
to my baby
would rather slide it
like a knife back up my spine

let it reach my skull
and blow   blow man
rather than give it
rather than give it
to my boy

CRY

When i could no longer cry
i held wet inside me
the leaky wound of death

once when it had no
place to go it flared up
pelting denial like a brick
my stomach a wasteland

i awoke reached
for the screaming teapot
hissing and misting my eyes

i want a new dress
red as these flames
that flare my eyes
and burn reality back into
the black of my hands

i've come late to a true
understanding of my sinister condition
my left arm half numb and prickly
this morning i'll pretend
these needles are not mine

afraid i'll burst
blow up doors little white haired ladies
on the F train
or screaming blond yuppie kids
on the caviar line in Balducci's

i run back inside
change into my pink lace blouse
put on lipstick paint my nails
adorn my hair with dragonflies

my eyes a carcass picked fresh
by tears a hesitant breeze moves
the thin white curtains
that speaks to me

will i always hear the windcalls
if i am slumped with tears and tea

i bury this blue month of pain
my heart blown open in rooms
where there are no doors no windows

there's a reckless breeze
an ocean at the edge of my skin
Cry

WATER

For Ronald K. Brown

Commissioned by Jacob's Pillow Dance Festival for Ronald K. Brown's EVIDENCE with additional funding from the National Endowment for the Arts

The Spirit   spirit of water
rides back of his kin
breaks his legs down
to dust   to mist

who is he   come to lie down
secret as blood
silent as scrubbed bones
come to steal the eye teeth
come to rob morning   from the saints faces

who is she dressed in white
with waist beads silver rings
and Florida water behind the door

A blue river ran past his teeth
a field of foxgloves and cosmos
Innocence walked down a dusty red dirt road that day
and the children threw rocks threw rocks
at his natty hair   at his natty hair

cry for our children cry of the children
we have come to claim Atlanta
we have come to testify to celebrate
what are you going to do
what are you going to do

long ago when days were light
and smelled of pork chops and honeysuckle

31

on a reverent morning
I walked into my daddy's sick room
and held his hands

I washed my daddy's feet
he wakes like Lazarus
raised up in bed my daddy smiled
kissed me with the half grown
needles of his face

my daddy smiled
his missing tooth grin
and all my world   all my world come undone
with my daddy's smile
my daddy read from the psalm   called me a saint

he smiled that smile
all da sun come rushin in   come rushin in
when my daddy grin
i knew it was my daddy
whagi sun it name
an all da rainbows wha God ever made
come to linger in my daddy's eyes

sweeter days   sweeter days
was in my daddy's feet
and we danced a blue river
a blue river
to the rice and cabbage crops
growin wild

and da smell of stew fish
and green bananas
walked out of ma mama's kitchen
lordy   lordy   be
better days was in ma mama's stew
was in ma mama's hips

ma mama's hips

and we danced a holy ghost
a holy feast
a water dance for peace
we stayed holding on
holding on to the salvation
the water and the blood

holy ghost i say amen
amen two times
what yu gonna do
what are you gonna do

i was standing there
i was standing there
me and sister holy ghost   sister holy ghost

and sky looked out it's gray window
then the rains came   the rains came
and i knelt to catch the crooked water
falling from her mouth
i knelt to catch the crooked water
falling from her mouth   testify

what are the names of our sons
names long like river
its skin the color of tea
rage like bloodied hands
long like the Chattahoochee
the souls of dead Black boys
linger long   join hands
and cry for mercy

cry for our children
cry of our children

what are the names of our sons
the sons we loved but failed
to protect   to protect
what are the names of our sons   Jesus
their fractured smiles
heavy vined like morning glories
under the brown wreckage of their eyes

lips blue and mauve like death
come smell the floral fragrance of death
the light aroma of sin
crawling all around our filthy hands

it was spring when morning came
clear and glorious upon the water
that day river slipped by us
rolling beige onto our flat faces
someone called   called the names of our sons
and ai cahn believe   cahn believe   all our sons

someone blew white rum
sprinkled water
and we jumped the broom
and shouted holy Jesus
he is here   holy in his resurrection

and water stood up
river slipped by us
we carry their weary bodies
we carry their weary bodies
inside our eyes like fireflies
so we never forget
never forget   never forget

outside water waits
to hold another   to rock another
to break his legs down to dust

to mist

what are you gonna do
death must wait until i am ready
i have three more lives before surrender
death must wait

all day i fry fish
boil white corn with bay leaves
blow white rum
tie six garlic cloves with white twine
light six white candles
to the gods for our sons

bring me the names of
our sons
so many sons

how does the body
attach itself to such grief
pain is a ring
slipped silver on my wedding finger
the music slow laid out like a flesh-embroidered sheet
feel the liquid under my feet
death must wait

sweeter days were young
when we danced a blue river
danced a blue river
called another name
till water moved over
givin way to baptism

death must wait until i am ready
i have three lives to live
before surrender

death must wait
i have three lives   and water to rock me
and i'll dance a blue river
dance a blue river
calling the names of our sons
the names of our sons
our sons   our sons   our sons

LETTER TO LOVE IN WINTER

Sharp in the crack of winter's brow
the lime leaves are stalk dry
shadows of a gray ache
shut close sun's mellow mouth

the ragged quilt of winter's light
fades with despair at four
how sorrowful his eyes
lying dormant next to mine
questions of a body
beats out a dull refrain

and now you've sent him
to my side
oh love what fond amusement
are you seeking from my heart

SUGAR

My pancreas was fretful
and never did work well
the day it finally gave out
it ambushed my entire planet

from hibiscus to orange blossom
from insulin shock to
hospital bed
the thud of ripe mangoes falling in thick mud

from nutmeg blurred eyes
to dusty charred shell
from penicillin to lantus
the ripe photographs of my life escaped
through old boarded up windows

my sugar house cracked and folded in on itself
part of my threshold gone forever
dear missing pancreas I love you
you strange and unforgettable bastard.

Convincing the Body

(2005)

Convincing the Body

Study your poems
when you think you're going crazy
lay naked on the earth
cover your shame with praise poems

cover the bright bay windows
curved around a cruel day
make curtains of your poetry

cruise the sky
cruise the sky
find that slight patch of sun

stack poems, two three five
at a time on top each other
add your tears
make a bewitching violet poultice
cover those wounds child

gather acacia leaves
a dash of sea salt
two unruly beams of light

two drops of blood
from one left hand wedding finger
a fountain pen
three diamond nibs
seven wads of paper

keep by your bedside
one flask kerouac
nine sprigs lorde
three june jordan candles
two tablets clifton

ten wads neruda
three large jars perdomo juice
forty-five reams Phife Dawg

brass skillet   two teacups
two steel pans
mountainous garlands of
ai ai ai

your reflection
study your reflection
use as mirror rain water
keep calabash full

trace your mouth
lips deformed and bleeding
praise that mouth and swear
swear to love yourself

study your reflection
watch your eyes
look for crossing buffalo
clear a path   ten quick breaths

your heart
strike your heart
strike it child
let it break   break

strike it
beat spontaneous poems
from wrist hips
lips fingertips

heartbeat violent
irreverent basin blue poems
beat poems from legs

chest   eyes   breast

now read   read
damn!   like a poet

First Hyacinth

Oh mother speak
your words written
on this brown paper bag soil

on the lower east side
red painted toes kiss sidewalk
of summer's gown

already the first hyacinths
spring a silver-blue song
a fragrant distraction

in flatbush Trini women
shimmer in halters
belly buttons beg questions of war

a flat black pencil
scrawls its name
across one determined eyebrow
secret gospels dance around each lid

PROMISE

The American soldiers
should not promise the children sweets
this morning I heard a story

yesterday a girl of war
ran to a soldier for sweets
one arm poised for embrace
his other arm bulged with
lucky charms

she splintered into teeth
arms brains   spleen bones
blew a white cracked wind
always in his dreams
in his dreams

Notes to the Gracious Earth

after she left
vinca and begonia
sang rowdy at my window
mountain offered her smoky blue frock

what if she'd stayed
I'd never see fever grass dance
in backyard stream

nor fresh mint
jump the neighbor's fence
hug the feet of red board deck

no country air rushing sweetly
through clothesline
arms outstretched awaiting hug

what if she'd stayed

no green pea splitting pod
no sparrow's frolicking beak
no forsythia to press her yellow thighs
through gaping smiles of front porch slats

no racing flame of moon's red mouth
to kiss this gaping earth

Rules of Goodness

open heart real slow
smile more, trust less, listen well
run when thunder roars

travel light and leave
anything too heavy, for
good heart to carry.

BLACK

1.
she be a Black woman
born between a town's whisper
and a slither moon

she be Ibeji woman
born in hard crop guava season
between calabash and casava
she be the dust of Arima mountains

2.
this skin is a black language
cadent and regal
brown of the cola nuts
from which all nations rise

3.
I carry the wail of tribes in my skin
my mouth jeweled with Africa
would lay down my life for
this black skin

this skin is a temple
where the gods meet
to shout perfection

MILK BREATH

Decades pass
then one day his face calls
from a peacock-colored frame
of a Ghanaian snapshot
right there on a dirty street corner
in Accra you remember the boy

you remember his milk breath
his hunger
his bony knees
pressed into your ribs

you remember how his sweet body
pushed against yours
until there was no air
only pulled skin impaled on a gnarled wrist

you remember how his little fist
beat against the door
beat against the door of your mother's womb
to save you both

and later
you sure hope
he took you in
hair, bone, spit, spine, spleen, split nails
knees, knuckles, ovaries, areolas

you take him deep
in the bough of your shoulder blades
deep in the pale straw of your palm prints
you fill up with the brown-nutmeg
curve of his newly formed elbow
his hollow prickly scalp soft along the center

you remember his love songs
sung in C minor
how he made you laugh
when he twitched his nose
into a tree trunk

pulled his eyes into long zippered slits
with teeth, bone and raised flesh
how he strummed your face like a guitar
until sleep settled in
then magga, like wings his legs
shelter, straddle, rock

later you remember
the slack blue flesh of his neck
the line-laced blue of his hands
damp and beautiful
like the underside of leaves

and you remember
blue this is why *blue*
yes, *blue* in any shade
became your favorite color
Iris and morning-glories
your favorite flowers

you remember the drunken cave
of his chest
the murmur-mad whistling
of his lungs

the warnings of how he'd take
you too if you didn't run
you remember his half-smile
the gray cloud-laced blink of his eyes

and the leaving
the letting go was simple
quick   still
his ear fanned graceful along
its curled stem crimson-pink
flushed with living

and in that moment you knew
you could bend like him
break like never

but the sea
the black earth sea soil
rose quiet to greet him
his eyes emptying into the
ocean's steam

and you furious, broken
retched mouth howling
pulsed with pebbles, seed, seaweed
fissures of moss-stained bones

wrecked with the stench of death
ache a white vat on your skin
tumble, widen in that vast
mountain of wind

MAKING A BOY

My belly swells as Mausica river
I wanted the cowry shells
to tell me you were a girl

this night I pray
river stays calm within its shoulders
not like that time
in a mad furor its wind like wings
plucked my Easter hat from my head
and gave it to river

I never got it back
whomever you are child
tonight I swear to let you keep your voice

a sweet clear ocean
pulls me to her bridal bed
the seed he planted
grows a love tree in my gut

breasts heavy sore
your father lathers them
with cocoa butter
he shakes out the doormat
lays blankets in the sun

fear welling up in his eyes
when I say   *it hurts to speak*

and from my thighs
fell two blue storms
one to clap and whirl
spin spill words
one to stand mediator before Oya

we buried your brother
later that day
earth was black
save for the moon

for five days straight
rain cursed the dirt
as did I
salt covered land
the bed where I labored

and from my tears
came your eyes
the loveliest shade of brown and red
tinged as Arima dust

I embrace my fortune
my son
your mouth an overflowing gourd
may your words never give warning
never give warning
never give warning of their coming.

TOBAGO

Up a trail of warm rocks
and bamboo shoots to the river
balisier like mad red dogs
open their slight yellow palms

when I open your palm
dark heirloom lines
map secret temples

sun a tilted teacup
spills her orange taffeta grin
upon the mocha earth

I could follow the siren lines
of your smoky spine anywhere lover
let me plant guavas in your hair
eat curried rice off your tummy

bind my arms
mount me slow
convince this body

vulgar rough defiant
if I cry I'll blame the poem
taking root inside me

night extends her bluish arms
blankets curved shoulders of trees
what mad delight washed us up
on this delicate bank
your thighs so Friday night

a thin glitter line outlines our frame
darling, have we scorched the river bank?

MANGO PRETTY

she fat
she cyan be pretty
if yuh fat fat fat no way in hell yuh could be
pretty

all she do is eat eat eat
how she could be pretty
no modern man eh go want she
only food food food
yuh cyan be pretty   pretty fat

look at she
big face
big teeth
big mouth
big tits
big tummy no
nonono   no way
she cyan be pretty
who go want she

de white man say say say
elle   *in style*   *essence*   say say say
ebony say say say   she ugly
new york times say say say   too fat fat fat
to be pretty

ah mean . . . long bouncy hairsmooth chin
light light light unblemished skin
uh huh pretty   pouty lips
straight nose   tiny ass   barbie feet
now that is pretty
white white white skinny skinny um pretty
ah mean

yuh could eat eat eat
bu yuh mus puke puke puke
then then then yuh could be pretty pretty
pretty
yes pretty   so slim and trim
and pretty

long hair straight nose   pouty lips
slight nigga booty
blue eyes long long braids blond braids
puke puke puke   pearly white skin puke

douche bag
ex-lax
diet tea skinny
losin   teeth size one size two bad breath
thin thin thin   is in
pretty pretty pretty
not fat like she size one size two
skinny skinny fashion skinny

eat eat eat   now now now puke puke
puke
now yuh prettyyes yuh pretty now yuh
pretty   yes yuh pretty
pretty pretty   pretty barbie

not fat like she
wid she food food food
so ugly
rice and peas
curry chicken
brown stew
fat fat fat chicken gravy

fry bake   saltfish
cocoa bread

crab and dumplin
white bread
callaloo pig feet
mutton chops
fat fat fat chicken gravy

she fat fat
and *know she pretty*
yes pretty   *mango pretty*
Black and sexy just ah . . . slight slight slight
bit nasty
big booty soft tummy for her baby
well round and full

island beauty
and dey greedy
cause dey grab she
just to taste she
and she big big big

sweet big big big
strong unruly fem butchy
big mouth big lips big arms big hips big
kiss

and she famous
love she food love she pretty love she poetry
love she mudder
big mouth
big ass
big brain
love she son love she daughter
love she friends
love she trees
quiet streets

and she big

damn big big money
big words
big heart
big love
big feet

and she big
yes big

damn big
da doh make she ugly

he say she fat an Black and ugly yuh know
just because   just because just because
she ain't skinny
why she cyan be pretty
who yuh to say she soooooooo ugly
to fat fat fat to be pretty

but she pretty
pretty pretty
pretty happy
big brain   big plans   big goals
big mouth   big tongue   big kiss

an de love she big heart big hands big soul
so what she big
yes big damn big
big big

so what she big
big big
fine big

she cyan be pretty

Arrival

(2017)

WILD SORREL

—if dem chiren hit me today
I go hit dem back what about you cherylallison,
what you go do

praise Dara's dare and her spell of words
praise my swift backhand and the girl that fell
tearing her ass wide   praise father
who did not tell mother

praise my shy girl learning to be tough
praise the dust and the girl that rose
praise the chest that puffed to bursting—
the chest raised with new breasts tucked in blue bra
praise the new breasts

it was love not poverty that made my first homemade bra
Mammie and Tanty Verna's hands buzzed
with the Singer sewing machine
they singing along to Calypso

one sister stopped to snap her fingers
shake her tiny butt
one ran the tap water a little 'til it ran clear
the other made the limeade   drank it without ice

one wiggled to young Elvis
he the new blue-suede-shoe crooner
they Black pony-tailed half-girls
bright red bindi in the middle of their foreheads
milk still warm in their green-mango breasts

a hip slung low beige piece of moon bright in her narrow dress
blue-corn silk ribbons holding breeze at bay
my Trinidad her red Ixora flush of dusk
her sugar-diabetes running wild

at nine the demon of menstrual cramps drummed all night
Mammie boiled wormgrass tea for pain
every Sunday bike rides tears
castor oil straight   and orange soda for chaser

years later orange soda would soothe my monthly cramps
its taste reminded me of my childhood mangoes
its center jellied and damp
as an inner womb readying
my ivory bowl for twin boys

blessed with twins
one would stand before Oya
the other would clap and whirl spin words

one would hear river talking
the other would write it down
one would change the world
the other would leave it

from wind's beak once fell two seeds
one a bird the other a girl
turned wild sorrel tree

ZUIHITSU ON EATING POEMS

At fourteen
I learn the ways of poetry
how it enters your heart then hands full frame

it works its way down the torso then out of the mouth
that glorious undeveloped mouth that only knows chapstick and girlish
giggles

a mouth unknown to beauty
still innocent to the delicious pineapple of a woman's kiss

At twenty
I fell out with my new husband of less than a year
my four-month-old son and I climbed into my mother's bed she held us
and read poems

Mom reads Gwendolyn Brooks   Georgia Douglas Johnson
she reads Derek Walcott   Léopold Senghor and Langston Hughes
something shifts at the magic of their songs

the husband calls and calls we do not answer
what holds me is this mystic doorway of words
and the rich hum of my mother's voice in the living room of these poems

a crop of words loop my heart there are
azaleas and hibiscus where the hurt
used to be

Hibiscus rosa
lowers blood sugar   lowers cholesterol
lowers blood pressure
prevents heart disease
its root soothes mucous membranes

Hibiscus flowers are also known as Jamaican sorrel

as a child in Trinidad I drank sorrel
in Jamaica I drank sorrel and ate poems

I decorate my windows with pink azaleas and red hibiscus
place hibiscus at the front door for abundance

I eat poems for breakfast
sprinkle some on my honeydew melon
on my Inca-red quinoa
I feed poems to my son he eats them
like heirloom tomatoes

Later when he is gone I make murals of poems
each painted with the Bulgarian-rose of tree bark
while the kettle hums I lure another string of words lithe like dragonflies
the wail of tribes ascending in the language of leaves

COMETS

My father draws a map
promises my mother the river
a mirror   pyramids
he grows her a lime tree   buys her a camel
and a white coat of lamb's hair

my mother sits on the steps of my father's house
her waist the size of his grandmother's gold bangle
he's given her this glowing gem for her twenty-fourth   birthday

under my mother's floral waistband
my twin brother and I keep ourselves secret
we read tea leaves to decide who will tell

my mother is the canvas
upon which father paints his ark
father is a rocket jets mother's heart

when moonlight softens the earth
they walk in each other's footsteps

my twin and I become comets
we lance them
we lance them apart.

THAT AUGUST

Did you know my mother
slight slip of a girl
hips a wooden washboard
hair a runaway kite

father did you know my mother
her half-Indian eyes bright as fireflies
her black majestic rain of hair
it was her flaming pride
did you know

a sharp muscular cry hurls the night
blood a red hat
knitted to braids and bone

news climbed the town like wildfire
father did you know my mother then
slight slip of a girl
garnets for eyes
mouth a cracked earth exploding.

The Sea at Marabella

Southern coast of Trinidad

I want the pound of ocean
by the sea in Marabella

I want my wooly fat braids
tied to flying ribbons flapping like bird wings

I want my stick thin legs
running after cousin Villma's bike

begging for a ride
mouth filled with salt air and nutty sand

I want the loose butts of old women
falling out of their too-small swimsuits

their eyes halfway hidden
under the rims of big panama hats

their french creole
spicing up the dead jellyfish air

I want to churn the wooden ice cream freezer
while the boys pack it with salt and ice

I want my Trinidad
her chest a finely sculpted bamboo bowl

her shoulders the bright jawbone of God
I want to feel the sting of hot sand

the pound of ocean
from my Marabella sea.

Poodles and Sour Cream

I am the third generation of daughters
whose mother worked as a domestic
in that Great Neck house of poodles and sour cream
girls younger than me
called my mother by a nickname

Genie, what's for breakfast
Genie, wash my hair
Genie, take my bike out
Genie, get my boots off

my mother who raised me to call elders
tanty, uncle, granny related or not
Tanty Evelyn, Tanty Vida, Uncle Dadoo, Uncle Horatio
even the bum with the limp was called Mister Broke-up-foot

in that cold New York house
my mother spent three years eating mashed potatoes
and sour cream doing sleep-in work
waiting for she green card to come

and every night crying for she beloved daughter
she could not care for while raising the white lady chiren.

I Name Gyal 3

My home name is gyal
I remember who I am braided gyal
drinking cocoa tea eating fry bake

I make sardines in onion stew
just like Mammie teach me
I remember who I am

I remember to say paliwal, not best friend

remember to say bodi, not string beans
remember to say melongen, not eggplant

zaboca, not avocado
remember to say, she bold face, fast an out-ah-place
remember I more bold than she

everybody say, so long you in America
you still have accent
I am the daughter of Elma and Roy
I name gyal, I say.

WORSHIP

She eats smoked almonds
slowly from my fingers
licks the pink Himalayan salt
from the bend of my palm
this is how worship begins.

Blue Heart Zuihitsu

Once we moved in my lover would wake in the middle of the night saying
babe my back is itching
I would brush her back   until she moaned and slept against the sloped howl
of night

this afternoon after the mammogram my breast still stings from the shit of a
machine
named after a woman   Imagine that
no woman would create a contraption that could cause other women such pain

I walked through the farmer's market along Adam Clayton Powell Plaza   the
     slight
pungent smell of fresh chard rosemary   rhubarb tickled my nostrils   I
     moved
in closer to soothe my ache

South of London
I walked down Eddy Grant's Electric Avenue, pass Brockwell Park
memories of Jay Day Cannabis Festival still hung in the trees
1960s tie-dye head wraps   cowrie earrings   floral bell-bottom jeans

In Brixton they recognize my Trini right away
Scotch bonnet peppers and jerk sauce on my tongue
my mouth tears into an East Indian mango

she said   *she gets angry when I'm sick—*

said   *she wants me to put on my big girl panties (the ones I buy in bulk at*
Duane Reade) and take care of my shit—

          last night she tore my skin that's right tore my skin
          she should have worn a muzzle for this vacation

in the water was a mirror   I saw the bruise of her words take
shape claws   then   knives

bruised my small black—

two days of silence followed   two days of silence

then my lover said
I don't really get angry
I get scared   *can you forgive me*
one
more
time   *forgive—*

I passed the lake   stood under the blueberry grove of trees

     hearts of berries stained the ground a deep blue

forgive me
she said

I tore my skin

     felt it open
exposed the dumb gnarled pulp

finally my heart turned
miss mermaid has weeds in her tail
there are adjectives up for sale

did I tell you I was a twin

     I cannot remember which self loved her so much
everyday   less   less
less everyday less every
day   love her   less

     I remember the year I took my girl out for an exotic father's day
     dinner
      she was the daddy of our house then

the next year for father's day I made a Trinidadian Pelau   with crab lobster
and pigeon peas

I wanted to make it an annual tradition—

scallions mint leaves   bits of mango chutney   rice in coconut milk and for
          desert
ginger watermelon with raw honey on top

I served it on our living room floor clad in bare feet   half an orange bugle
          beaded
sari   and my blue-fish-eyed bindi

—on the kitchen counter

          the glass table
the bathroom floor   holy god

praise tenderness
the sickle moon of her
bent against the bedside lamp

still stops my heart.

TOOLS

A woman's body has everything in it
to save her life

if you must
use your legs as raft

heel as hammer
teeth as machete

monthly blood as healing salve
milk for building

breasts as shelter
learn to breathe

use your locks to suture every wound
learn to scream

learn to scream
learn to speak

learn to live
within the smallest muscle of your heart.

Toco

The unfinished house in Toco
my father took me to the summer
I still loved him

walls still unhung he draped
a sheet so I could change into my swimsuit
his limbs bamboo slim

he made ginger lemonade
and sweetened it with ole talk
and fresh orange slices

the unfinished house in Toco
where later I waited
for his 1960's green Desoto
to round the coast,

waited for a postcard
the wonder-of-the-world leaf
grew roots in my notebook,

I waited for the flared crowing of his voice
across water,
the bend of his arms around my neck
a ruby necklace to be worn.

ROY

For my father

All he had left:
his tamarind-polished limbs
gaps between the squares of his teeth

the sea is a collector of dreams
what I would not give for his browning bark of fingers
the lives between those sequined bones
his garnet and silver wedding ring metal beaten flat

what I would not give for the selfish dust
in his laughter
the precious copper of his tongue clacking

morning   the gone moon
picks at these blue-cadmium bones
my porcelain beak of body rises
I become window
frame.

In This Pure Light

Zuihitsu for a son

I.

October 2008

We are in the hospital waiting room at
University of California in San Francisco
my son is about to have a kidney transplant
my daughter-in-law is the donor

      a dear friend gives my daughter-in-law a silver necklace
from it hangs three pearl-shaped hearts   for love
strength   and hope
I ask to wear the necklace during surgery

2.

November 1970

Dear son
On this joyous morning sheets still smell of birth
our newborn inheritance between us
still an unburned bride my body blooms
become river   boat   village   grave
your small mouth sewn to my blue flesh   glows

your twin brother
gone to meet the breath of God
waiting in that field of light

son
    you are my pillar tree wealth straw-broom looking glass   wings scream
    temple

fire
      break the nightlight the city   love

      does the organ of the heart shiver in this pure light
or does the light shiver in the presence of the heart

3.

I so want love
      can this dyke-mama body absorb all that light

bombastic red
I rouge my mouth

ease out the door
my tightest dress   the green brocade
piano plays

4.

June 1985

The house on Merrick Boulevard
my son's dad tells him I am a lesbian

he screams and cries roars his rage
earth hums with ache
one snapped tree broken at its center
he is fifteen   my son a kiss slips from my palm
I fear this death more than I fear my own

pain has slimmed me

the next few years I grow a Judas body   a false tongue
   my eyes a watercraft for the Gods

my son grows narrow in the damp of boyhood
   the questions of his body a crooked dirt road
much later he becomes a spell maker
      I adore his sensitive words

5.

Last night on the phone my son hums me one of his new tunes
tells me   *I always knew I'd be a rapper of positive thoughts*
he tells me   *I*   *love my grandmother*   *but when she tried to pray*
my hip hop
         dreams
away
I would repeat in my head   *I will have my music*   *I   will   have   my*
music
         someday I
will   I   will

his body became a temple for hip hop

When I found out my son was a diabetic

I wished to make his curse mine   inside I burned with blue
shame   I had
         given him bad
sugar
I had given him my diabetes

four needles   four shots of
insulin
four shots of insulin   a
handful of pills
that's what it takes to make my body work each day
four Peri exchanges   that's
what it takes for my son's body to work each day

Mother's Day 1999

my son calls to say
he needs a kidney

6.

That night I beg God to give me the burden   forgive my sins
is it because I love a woman
God
I make a pact
God
I swear I will—

7.

there's blood on my knees
I paint my face holy
the color of white apple blossoms   I make another pact with God

8.

On the flight from Brooklyn to Oakland   I pray and pray
my son is getting sicker   I don't know how to comfort him/me

     My grandson David   meets me at the airport
     he hops on one leg all the way to the baggage carousel

I'm gonna give Malik my kidney   he says
I will   *I*   *will*   *I'm not scared ah nothin—*
he is eight

We go directly to the hospital my son is asleep
I sit at his bedside and wait
two a.m. the phone rings   my girl is on the line
how did the test results go   she asks

we are quiet for a long time

My son stirs
I drop the phone   I hug my child I hold his hand in mine
kiss him
rub his head   squeeze him   squeeze him
until he says
ouch   ouch   ouch   ma

Arrival

An elegy

on the day I arrive my best friend Rodlyn will wake early and sweep the drain
in front   she little trinket shop   she will put all the blue-sequined bracelets
and silver scarves up front   she knows I will try them on first
blue green yellow   then pink

Mom will peel a few grapefruits   those huge pink-skinned ones
      they sweeter than them   *pale*   *wash-out whitey ones yuh know*
that's her way to point up her feelings for white folks   not too veiled   not
    too brash

she will fix my favorite peanut punch add a dash of rum   the rum really for
    she
but she go pretend it for me

           my father will try to put his arms around her   she will
           say *look*   *leave meh alone yes*   *mister*
           she will take a few sips of the peanut punch then get back to her
hat making   peacock blue and yellow felt bound by a black shiny crushed
    velvet band

my father will put on coffee   he will sit on the front porch   chin in right
    hand and greet
every big bottom women walking by

once I get settled mom will come to my room and present me with my felt and
    velvet hat
amid tears and kisses she will say
what took you so long to come   *Cheryl*   *I missed yuh*   *everyday*   *missed yuh oh*
God

she will say   *how's*   *Malik meh darling boy*
and yuh lady-friend Ceni   *yuh still wid she and Cheryl why yuh wearing blue eye*
shadow

whakinda color is that
who tell yuh it pretty
yuh didn't find de right color for yuh pretty dark complexion in de store
but is not everything them thief selling for yuh to buy   yuh know gyal

*   I thought I   teach you better*
anyway never mind all that   I have so much to tell yuh lord

Cheryl yuh see your father   that man eh change

MOONFLOWER

In four weeks mom you will be dead four years
what more shall I make of your secrets and the dried flower petals
left in the pocket of your good dress

once the full moon opened my father's palm
released his umber-brown rage
on my eighth birthday daddy twisted my step mother's arm
right in front of me
she howled in pain then sent me to the store

chocolate ice cream
she said   *get chocolate in a cone*   *keep the change   keep your dress*
clean
your mother wants you to keep your dress clean

later when she tucked me in bed she whispered
never marry   never marry   never marry a man afraid of his own face

back at home
when I told mom
she became an open bible
a Psalm of David   she became Psalms 101.3
                  I will see no wicked thing before mine eyes:
she became a crack in the back door
her family geography   their dialect of sorrow
she became the bearer of her mother's secrets and her mother and her
mother before her
I want to scatter mother of pearl upon the stunned earth
somewhere a daughter pines for her mother
her mother a steep hill wired with ghosts

what
shall
I
make

of your secrets
and the dried flower petals
left in the pocket of your good dress

my father's cigarette lights the small bedroom

    I imagine a heavy heart growing inside
day smells of magic the vice of dawn moans like djembe drum.

remember when joy lingered

    mom's breast is weeping
the baby's receiving blanket smells of stale seaweed
mom wants the earth to echo cries of her blue newborn son

             womb a shattered cup sits on its rusted frame

with his baby boy gone dad moves on
he turns to the stout woman in the tight red dress

mom tends her citrine-yellow dahlias and her plump baby girl
her arms lean stalks of sugar cane

daddy brings a basket of goldenrod mangoes to my first grade class   we smell
    the hot
road and the sea salt in them   soon the school song freezes in our mouths and
    our voices
go astray   we taste the sap and sugar fruit warm like breast milk
high in our summer mouths

daddy I was hoping to make you a garland of seaweeds for your gleaming
    neck   a burlap
sack of dried fruit

I am my father's daughter   restless
with no August breeze   I   become a borrowed day

mom loves extra high heels   a milliner who makes hats by the midnight
breath of her oil lamp
at fifteen
I sneak into my mother's closet and wear her leather boots and expensive
dresses to school

she becomes a deep throat brass band

quiet, please
grandmother pleads in her soft French-patois
        I float in and out of the music of her breath
        the way I float on my mom's back at the beach

on Sundays our kitchen smells like bok choy and ginger-salmon
mom sets the table for just us two
she recites her poems loudly   sun following her waistline around the room
her body a pulpit   her mouth calls to ecru-blue mountains
calls balisier   bacchanal and wayward tree

once I placed a bunch of red and orange hibiscus blossoms on mom's night
    stand
I wanted her to observe the delicate way they broke skin
pushing ever so slightly into
the vortex of the room

                mom held her/my secrets deep in the ruby socket of her heart

    I will not forget the amethyst-blue corridors of your voice mother
your burnt-sienna fingers on my back like guitar strings

four years of missing you has made the small delicate bones of my spine into a
    church

        last night in my dream I tried to call you
what I wanted to say—
to say was—

what kind of birthday cake would you like this year

      remember the year I bought
you a strawberry cheesecake   laughter slid off your jasper-brown skin

all night it rains
in the morning my forehead flush to the window
                        mom holds something out to me
a braid of moonflowers
and her arms.

Mama Phife Represents

(2021)

———————————

The Summer Phife Was Born

The year Malik was seven I was a theater major at York College in Queens. When I could not afford a babysitter, I took him with me to class, poetry readings, and rehearsals. He would sit quietly and watch us rehearse, but mostly he would run around and play at the back of the theater. It was there he met Imani, the little girl who was his best friend until the day he died. After playing for hours, I would ask him to settle down and write a poem, which he did cheerfully. His first poem was about being in the park after dark. A bit scary, but he had spent many hours at the park with his dad playing soccer, often into the late evening.

As a teenager he told me that he thoroughly enjoyed expressing himself on paper, and that it helped him to understand his questions more clearly. I felt overjoyed because I was raising a Black man in troubled America who was seeking answers for some of his issues and questions.

The summer Malik was ten we were making plans to send him to YMCA summer camp in Jamaica, Queens, again when he told me how he hated that camp and did not want to go anymore. He had spent three previous summers there and seemed to really like it. I wanted to know why he didn't want to go anymore. He told me that the children fought and cussed a lot and that he'd rather stay home with his grandmother. She was a lot of fun and they did things together like visit family, shop for fruit, study his bible lessons, and cook. They even went to vacation bible school together. I knew lots of playtime was secretly woven in between the lines of that righteous listing, so I made him a scrapbook and asked him to record his thoughts and send me a note every day telling me how he was and what he was doing. The first note went something like: "Malik played in the hot sun today, scrimmage and baseball, then he rested with a cool piece of watermelon. Grandma got stung by a bee and Malik did too." That was the beginning of a series of letters, journal entries, poems, and songs he wrote to his dad and I that year.

I will always believe Phife was born that summer

WHEN HER CHILD DIES

For Malik

A mother does not know her heart
will leap out of her chest

with such force
it will cause a rebellion

she does not know
that her hands will be numb for weeks

she does not know her sugar will rise
even though she has not eaten in two days

she will come to distrust her universe

her black-eyed Susans her sweet Williams
the soil she loves to squish her toes in

sun hugging her aching shoulders
moon scurrying across her worn windowsill

she will mistrust them all

when her child dies
friends will come daily with milk honey

cheese red wine spelt bread & ginger jam
she will not remember their touch

only their eyes glossed over with tears
she does not know

she will stop speaking to his father
and threaten to sue him

her hair will fall out in clumps
she will lose big spaces of memory

when her child dies
a woman will fight for her sanity

she will travel to Anguilla
beg Yemaya to bring him back

as the ocean swells
she will listen for his laughter

she will press her face in the damp earth
call his name

Malik
Malik
Malik Izaak

STITCHED

I've stitched your breath to my throat
child did your last howl resemble mine?

all day I want to sit in ashes
all the stars have followed you

since you've been gone

this left hand has betrayed me
has grown into my mother's

my index finger so crooked
it refuses to wash clean the dinner dishes

my eyes too are disobedient

I've told them not to tear
at the wound of the name son

does it listen?
did I say how lost I am?

your mom has a pacemaker Malik
that rebuilt heart too makes promises

it will rescue me will sing pretty
will rebuild the heave and steam of my body

each night takes a thigh   a breast   a begging skull
an arthritic knee

all around there are unhinged bones
wailing at the lip of sea

*

I miss my child's morning voice as I wake him on his birthday miss the way he says:

> *Ma tell me about my twin brother/and what time was I born Ma/and*
> *how many pounds did I weigh again/and when did you get to hold me*
> *Ma/how long did I live in my incubator/and tell me Mama the story*
> *about how I was born first/before my twin Mikal in the labor room/*
> *and how the doctors scurried around when they heard the loud hollering*
> *baby A/and how they came to find baby B on his way out/after you had*
> *told them repeatedly that you were a twin/and that you were having*
> *twins/how did you know this Mama/tell me Ma how you and Dad*
> *threatened the doctors/that you'd sign me out of Mary Immaculate Hospital/that you'd*
> *take me home without consent/take me home because I*
> *was yours/because my crib was ready/with the white blankets/the white*
> *curtains/the blue heart-shaped pillows Grandma sewed/and the rocking*
> *chair Dad painted white/*

Tell me Ma

APRICOT BEGONIAS

The week of the burial

1.

Two months after my son's death my friend Sabrina buys us tickets for
Mexico City   she says we are going on a pilgrimage to visit Frida Kahlo
She is fluent in Spanish   says she will take care of me   every evening
she makes ginger tea and hugs me tight
       She finds us an Airbnb in a small scenic art district   three times
we get locked out before we learn the key combinations   in the middle
of the living room there's a hammock with a view of the bridge   ahead
of the fog we see Mexico City rising in the distance   I've come late to this
grief
       We visit Frida in Coyoacán   At Lomas Verdes in an open square filled
with children and women wearing colorful off-the-shoulder dresses we listen to
folk music   and men dressed in charro suits singing *Besame Mucho* We eat
tostadas frijoles authentic mole chicken flautas with ceviche and guacamole
       Watch the body bend and curve   watch it shudder watch the body
an endless aching fire giving twin souls back to soil   I have not spoken in
days

The begonia leaves have grown small white dots   *sorry for your loss honey*
did you remember to blow out the white candles?   *honey did you dust the*
Tribe Called Quest CDs?   the guests will want to see them   have we called
the funeral director maybe we should sage the house
       I forgot   did you find a frame for it   the poem I mean the poem

2.

Apricot begonias are my favorite flowers   will you hold my hand love?

we marry in the middle of all that sorrow   after twenty years she is my wife
did we order begonias
                        are spider mums in bloom?
       baby, shall we order fresh Long Island peaches for the repast?

92

WIFE   wife   my wife the wedding cake has two tiers   we
dance to Beyonce's *Love on Top*   the guests join in we walk each other
down the aisle   we have never been happier   wife   wife   I
follow her around and scratch for something to pray to   I follow her like
a flock of wild turkeys   all my cells looking for something to hold to cling
to belong to
     baby turkeys are called poults   my baby is called too soon
     female turkeys are called hens will you hold my heart up to the light
beards on male turkeys are called gobblers   grief on a bride   is
called
     Will you make me a cup of rooibos tea with acai berry   cup of wild
sweet
     orange   are we expecting company should I fold the throw rugs?
fluff the sofa pillows?   will we serve South African Malbec?
     sorry for your loss   your   for loss

93

3.

The poets come to our home   with sage white candles and Florida water
they bring white calla lilies my son's favorite flower   they bring drums koras
and shekeres   they make a joyful noise form a prayer circle   Elana
leads all in song   we hug each other   a laying on of hands
we howl and pray together   I feel lifted

       Harmattan something close to lightning and sand-
   storm

did we remember to turn off the bathroom light?   In Trinidad we put the
top tier of the wedding cake in the freezer   save it for one year   have
you had anything to eat?

   Will you bring my writing pen and paper?   will the robins return
for grain?   is the door locked will everyone leave before sunrise?
what day is it? has the cat been fed?   use the good dishes in the glass
cabinet love   will I see my son again? can I?   On his first walk after
transplant surgery Malik walks to his wife's room   she has given him her
kidney   we love our kidney baby   we love Deisha

   Malik sends me purple irises for my birthday   *Mom I found my girl she
reminds me of you* What time will the funeral cars be here   will you put on
the kettle?   will we begin with the flutes of Carlos Nakai or Bob Marley?

4.

Will you pray with me?   I go to Yemaya
Jesse and Eric meet me in Anguilla
we listen   waves lick the sand like an obedient lover   we have fried conch and
lukewarm eggnog   at dinner the mixed drinks are weak   flies
never leave the table   the Black and white couple next door talks too
much   all night incessant talking and bragging   we laugh in odd places
don't hear a word they're saying   there's dried toast no milk for cappuccino
we discuss the poems of aracelis girmay read letters from Frida to Diego
love the dialect of Michelle Cliff in *Land of Look Behind*   in the morning
we search the island for fried bake and bacalao   we look for a wicker

frame for my new poem   night rolls in heavy as sorrow   my twin sons
Malik and Mikal are the butter yellow butterflies who greet me every morning
they walk me to the breakfast shed

Mom I need a kidney   will you lay with me?

dear mountain my heart is still not healing

I fill the bathroom with begonias and baby's breath   my bath water
is so hot it makes me   weep

where has my son gone   why did he leave I love it when he   calls
me Mama Phife calls me gal and boo   calls me Mama and Mami once
when he was twenty I told him he could call me Cheryl   he said hell no
imma call you Mama   and Sista

                    Watch the body bend and curve   watch it
                    shudder watch the
body this gift an endless aching fire giving twin souls back to the land

5.

Mom Deisha and I have a son   his name is David   Mom I am so in love
with that little guy

    Mom can I get in bed with you   Mom
I   don't   think   I'm   gonna   make   it
    I held that knife inside thought it would kill me

    Mom thank you for your unconditional love and guidance
    you have always stood by me Mama Sista
    I love you like no other—

sorry for your for your   losssssorry
your loss   tonight I want to hold the rain

my mother bury she husband who fall from heart attack in de morning
and my mother bury she second chile, a son, who fall from heart attack dat
evening my mother bury both ah dem next day and not one time not one time she
even ask the earth why
    sorry for your loss   says Fitzroy the cab driver who took me to the ferry in
Anguilla   With these tears I have made war
sorrow a blue Angel crashing against my teeth   grief is a dangerous
widow forgetting names of   To walk alone   t h e
deep side of river I think it's Monday   are the neighbors here?   *s o r r y*
    I have come to love Maker's Mark   honey when will the sun return?
three shots of whiskey   Cheryl Allison, age thirteen, leaving
Trinidad
    1964 arriving alone to New York City my parents no longer speak to
each other   Dad takes me to the airport   holds my hand
Mom lost somewhere in that hospital bed *sorry*   praise the daughter in
me and the brave son who carries my poetry   praise   him

96

6.
Cerulean color of Swazi Gods
After our son's death
we poured colored sugar over our cereal to keep our love sweet

7.
My daughter-in-law and I bring our arms full of grief to Annie's massage table
it is in a sweet cottage on the grounds of the lavish Coronado Hotel on the
West Coast
where Marilyn Monroe filmed *Some Like It Hot* in 1958
    You lay on Annie's table soft eucalyptus and bergamot oils fill the room
    Annie says let me shift your sorrow and mama just cry cry mama
    outside pregnant women walk the beach with mothers sisters lovers
    a chicken coop brood of children
    you watch a one-year-old boy take his first steps he tumbles over with
each half step he gets up grins tumbles again his screeches fill the impossible
length of ocean
    Once at the beach in Tobago we made paper boats sailed them
    to God knows where
    damn Malik   I thought I'd have you forever
    to be that small boy walking for the first time   red shirt blue overalls
    bald head   three shiny new teeth

    could not go to the site to bury the body
    hold me
    I fear I'll never speak again
    finally my lips apart   hissing

*

Our brilliant boy of four hosting his first birthday party,
Mom and Dad, he said, I want to host my own birthday party

Later he told his friends:
ladies and gentlemen, fasten your seat belts
And later:
Are you having fun, so how yuh likin' de party?

The summer before your death
I ate mostly cherries and watermelon in honor of the fruits you and Grandma
loved
Half-heartedly worked on the new book   drove you crazy with calls about what to
title it   we make suggestions found reasons to throw them out
How about—
In This New Light
I change the name three times before sending it to press
We settle on Arrival in honor of the places we have arrived in life

Seven months later I am a mother without her child
What is the term for that?

APRIL 5, 2016

I thrash around in bed
scream at the window
rage in the shower

I wonder if God hears

I look to Privet
her lean brown frame
she gives me no answer   just stands there
winking in her forest-green eye shadow
wordless the mask of her stillness
visible on her tapered neck

I eat and eat from the table of loss

finally when it's all gone I want more
afraid to live with/without it   I
miss the daily discipline of tears as company

miss the scorch
loss brings to my face
and please   the morning stab of grief

Memphis, Tennessee April 4, 1968
The day Martin Luther King Jr. was killed
New York City, April 4, 2016
I buried my child
I didn't notice until two weeks later
how could that be

HAND OF THE MIDWIFE

After Grandma Ada

My grandmother was a village midwife
not certified she delivered babies
shaped heads   broke fevers   flowed milk
buried umbilical cords and blue babies
a mix of Blue Cohosh raspberry leaves
Clary sage skullcap root
Viburnum opulus   goldenseal
my grandmother's right hand was a sure shot it patched broken hearts
dried turmeric leaves to improve digestion
boiled tamarind leaves to treat jaundice and diabetes
it scrubbed and ironed until
it was stiff and sore   Grandmother

what medicine plant can I boil for this wounding

Last Words I Said to My Son

baby I love you
I am so sorry you have to suffer so much
I've always loved you and those little boy pictures
Mami loved your little mischief self
I have a new collage of you near my bed

you do? he asked
take a screen shot and send it to me Ma
okay I will when I get off the phone
I love you
love you too Ma
sistren chuckle . . .

I miss my knight   miss my Phife
I would have preferred to take all his suffering
all his pain so he could stay

I am so grateful for that big love granted me

that's what imma say
when God comes to get me

You Ibeji Son

You Phife Dawg
You mas camp
You run dis muver boy
You Phife Diggy
You Funky Diabetic
You Don Juice
You Mutty Ranks
You first line ah verse
You big riff

You Diggy Dawg
You home house
You soca-hip-hop
You Ali boxing glove   Wop
You 33 LP
You Trini Gladiator
You Rhythm Kids
You DrPepper
You fig leaf
You preemie
You we are learning to live without

You Cheryl boo
You mama Ibeji
You peritoneal slugger
You Mt. Pleasant river
You cutlass
You broom
You broad pot spoon
You poui blossom
You pong plantain
You cassava pone
You shekere
You Five-Footer

You Knicks man
You in Claire's with Kaliya
You tossing son in air
You Deisha man
You David poppa san
You Walt main man
You first yu hear meh
You Volta River
You Elegua
You fit my heart

You suck-meh-teeth preacher
You Taiwo firstborn grandson
You of Elma/Ada/JadooMadoo/
Rufus/Roy
You bridge torn down rebuilt
You Ventilation
You Bend Ova
You machete
You twin
You mama twin

You Cheryl big son
You praise
You chant
You word ONE
You won
You job done
You Phife no drum
You live on
You done flipped da world

We Are Not Wearing Helmets

(2022)

———————

WE ARE NOT WEARING HELMETS

Miss Fannie your voice will weave my words into Congo drums
if I painted my face it would not be the color of surrender
cobalt blue like God's great sky before a rainstorm

not much in this country reminds me of myself
the billy clubs are coming Fannie
already the bombs have begun to fall

will the oppressors place those dull coils of smoke
around their necks
or sell it back to us as precious jewels

I have no more rage poems
was it something my father did
or was it Eve

we have become things to toss
plastic grocery bags the *Sunday Times*
old rusted beach chairs
cigarette butts

we are not wearing helmets or protective suits
the dead are coming Garvey
killers and liars too

outside hyacinths are shrieking
not loud enough to drown the screams

three a.m. moon
a voyeur through sheer blue
curtains of our bedroom window

the lush brown village of her
body creased around mine.

No More War Poems

For David Armstrong

I came home to find my door unlocked
not much in this country reminds me of myself
no bodegas mangoes affordable apartments
no tamarind Jarritos in Bed-Stuy
only Starbucks   Whole Foods   fancy wine stores
nannies   white girls with pit bulls and kombucha

America usta be my dream camp
my golden shoes

I wonder how we will carve this
what sharp knife shall I leave my grandson
somebody please touch this bright bone of longing

was there something important we gave up last year
there are no more war poems
we are not wearing helmets or protective suits

If I die this year love
only love will have her way.

Pigeon Point, Tobago

the lifted arms of market lady shine
with the pink and silver glow of fish scales
men with matted locks smile
through half-eaten cigars
teeth the color of black coffee

smells of crab and dumplings
sneak into the cracks of our louvered doors
noon and tourists hide under coconut trees
waiting for sun to shift
their half-lives weighted with rum punch and sun block

the high-pitch voice of market lady calls
fresh fish fish fifteen dollars ah pound
fish fresh fifteen—
five dollars　　　　　　that's it　　　　shouts
a vacationer from beneath a shady tree
twelve　she counters

six and you clean and cook it he yells
no man
lord have mercy
mister I have chiren to feed yuh kno　　　*I have chiren*

six dollars and not a penny more, he fumes

okay　　　　　*a'right*
six dollars fer de pound
and I clean and cook it

When Sky Fell

Always my grandmother's
belt her rage swift and painful

she'd throw a rock or shoe or
book if she called and you didn't answer

my mother's glitter arms
her fish body slicing water

once I fell asleep on her back
in a river that glowed and grew sweet lemons

her orchid wreath of wet locks
glowing when the sky fell

and if i say *father*
how can I unload that

father son wishbone
ghost or back of my knee

drunk willful womanizing
what we lost that year

after begging for months your father offers six dollars
for your week at summer camp

I was happy
had been for a long time

until he said
tell your mother I'm no money tree

his fist a small prickly pomerac in my
throat a husky chimney hanging from his mouth

here is your father
selling all your secrets

here is your father
facing you down like a woman

ten and staring down shame
could not look at cousin Avi standing next to me

then the crude boat of my lips opened
tripping the skeletal frame of my teeth

and me neck thrown back
hollering from my big Ochun mouth
fuck you into the red traffic of my island

June Plums

My father is forever my child
when I arrive in Trinidad he begs for bread and wine
he begs for new crisp American dollars
and a white shirt for his sister's funeral
at sixteen he begs me to ask my mother to take him back
even though he loves another woman
he loves my mother more   he says
my father shows me a picture of a small freckle-faced child
swears me to secrecy
promise that I will not tell my mother about the boy child he's hiding
he takes me to the ocean to meet my little brother
August sea still warm
I make a necklace of
seaweeds for his gleaming neck
my father thanks me for the boy's gift
throws himself into my arms
rage eating me like June plums.

Wonder if he loves this light-skin boy more than me?

GLORY

Most days before he was born
sun refused to leave her doorway

smells of nutmeg, Angostura bitters
and her own dust peppered the hallways

thyme, eucalyptus, lucky leaves   and small
reels of blond cobweb thread lined the bedside table

she had spent most of the nine months before his birth
sewing little white hats, sleeping gowns

booties and blankets. It seems like that boy housed her body
for ten months or more, and by the time he was born none of her

handmade fineries could fit him. Finally her water broke
streaking a patterned ribbon along the bathroom and hallway floors

it was a strange color, the midwife said,
a mix of pink pomerac and dark Chablis

oh God, spare him, she prayed as she waited
in the bamboo rocking chair that her grandfather had lacquered

the color of dried rosemary leaves. From the second-floor balcony she could
see the family graveyard elegant mansions of ochre and lime

she greeted Pa every morning with rose hips and brandy
sprinkled on the raw earth, and every night two white Oya candles

keep my boy well Pa, lord she had so many names
for that one child Asah and Rufus, Marley and Anslem

he was born when Sunday slipped behind the moon
into the wide oval verandah of the midwife's arms

III

puce was the color of his skin
she called him Glory.

MAMA

A child at my house calls me mama
he's placed moon in my ear
who is that girl who births a son
to hip the world
to name him sweetness
finally I have become wise woman
an oasis of wild fish
cut and scored by my Arima red-dirt hands.

BRAVE

For Ceni

Our bed grows lions and weeping willow trees
two crows nest with hatching frizzle fowls inside
Shelly the cat gives me the side eye
she can never find her food dish
it's over run by potted plants

again this week we are out of Fancy Feast
our socks mismatched
most of them have run away from home
the fridge is sparse 'cept for garlic knots
and fried rice

so many smart books on the shelf
begging to be read
now they cuss and look away from
the African village of fertility dolls poking out
their dusty chests

our sofa grows quilts and bamboo pillows
a fancy bird glass from Ikea
this morning I fell over the broom
with the ninety-cent dustpan attached
damn no Tiger Balm   one more pain patch on the shelf
we need to toss a coin for that

the kettle hissing on the stove
one hardboiled egg for breakfast
a fancy crystal tray filled with dust and address labels
let's just be brave and throw it all away.

LAST EUROPEAN TRIP I TOOK WITH MY MOTHER

On the road from Amsterdam to Stresa, the Italian fishing port where Hemingway once stayed, my mother and I oooohed, moaned and waved at the fields of sunflowers growing lush and thick. They seemed to wave back, bowing and racing the white light that hugged the bust of windows speeding to gorgeous Lake Maggiore on the edge of the Italian coast. Someone said they grew them in abundance to make sunflower oil. We were in awe of their toothy grins and must have passed two million of them, each more beautiful than the next, each more exotic and tempting than the other. I tried to count them, all lined up like soldiers in their yellow helmets. In that parade we passed so many viewing stalls for weddings, conceptions, christenings, and funerals, their dark heads blush and ready for birth. We were broken up that year, love, still my mouth watered for your breast.

You my sun god with stem erect and brown reminding me of your long proud neck gleaming with sweat after each evening's romp.

SAY HER NAME: BREONNA TAYLOR

For Breonna Taylor, killed by police in her home

That last summer in Liberty we made paper
boats sat our troubles and sailed them in the lake
we laughed like school girls
our dream a fingertip's distance away
we did not know our world would get so ugly

we did not know hundreds of Black mothers doing days work killing themselves
did not know sisters getting raped in the name of marriage
we did not know sixteen-year-old Gynnya McMillen
who died alone in a juvenile detention center in Kentucky
because she refused to remove her sweatshirt

we did not know Mya Hall a Black trans woman killed
alleged to be driving a stolen car
did not know Meagan Hockaday mother of three girls
killed in her home by police responding to a domestic issue
did not know Breonna Taylor killed by police in her home

we did not know Sandra Bland
Rekia Boyd
Kisha Michael
Tanisha Anderson

Shantel Davis
Miriam Carey
Eleanor Bumpers
did not know   did not know   did not know

we did not know
even the Catskill Mountains
with her wide embrace could not save us
we did not know to take a selfie of each other's ache

Black woman your heart is everything I believe in
your breath is enough
to save this trembling earth

may sun wrap you in her glitter gold sari
may the wind drape your head in bright orange heliconias
may we never cease to call your name
call your name
call your name

Here's an apology for your legendary life

You Braid Your Hair

the day after your mother's passing
you wash her clothes
shop for her burial outfit
a peach linen blazer
white lace blouse
white tea-length prairie skirt

social security freezes your joint account
next day her renewed driver's license comes in the mail
you take the LIRR to deliver her clothing
fall to pieces when the conductor says *St. Albans*
that was always your meeting place
she always picked you up there

you've lost her insurance policy
New York Life refuses to release her burial check
for thirty-eight years she paid down that damn bill
that's most of your son's life
when you finally find it they still won't cut a check
say they must notify the beneficiary first

you give away your mother's table, chairs, bed
you sign the thank-you cards
you can't mail them
after all they're not wedding invitations

you say *thanks so much* you cry a lot
wear your mother's sunglasses and sweater
use her old glasses at poetry readings

months later you unbraid your hair pack a weekend bag
life wears your drunk cave like a tin crown
hollow and pretty   you fill the corners
of each room with bitter bright marigolds
Mexican flowers for your dead.

LET'S MAKE A DRUM: LET THERE BE SINGING

I walk into the new apartment
throw white wine in corners for my dead
a panorama of light pulls me to the windows tall and bright this warms me
yes yes finally I found my place this mad city has worn me down I run so fast
I become tree stump when I awoke from sleep my hair was straw my poem
was the small child killed last week
I flew became purple martin ate mosquitoes and small fish

In our month of words we shared and shed fear skin rage sex flamed like
        bonfire
I don't want to have regrets but how I wish I was still that girl pulling petals
        to make bouquets feathers to make hats voices to make choirs
let's not exoticize poverty or privilege it ain't need no savior
in fact girl your glass ceiling hangs as low as fucking mine let's make a
family
        family
family   cook love   love
            love soup corn straw and poems

get me beet soup a chorus of birds
and a white obeah shawl while we wait for beauty
let's make a book a palace to dance in
fruit to feed our young
let's make a continent a kite let's make a drum
a knife a hymn a torch a chant
Ibeji waist beads Ndebele neck rings let's be tribal let's cook and seduce
let there be singing and sweet melons for summer let's make America better
than we found it let's dig up our bantu drums steelpans koras our ancestral
voices stronger than they left them
holla let our words read palms throw cowrie shells predict futures with tarot
        cards
let's pray and make babies daughters let's make blood who knows better than
        us how to do that

The Limitless Heart

(2020-2022)

Quarantine 2020

By nine am I've cleaned
doorknobs light switches faucets
iPhones with alcohol

I've washed the grocery packaging
wiped the fridge door tv remote
insulin pens sink hands

cleaned chicken for dinner
paced living room kitchen three times
washed doormats entry doors

scolded my love
for going to get cigarettes
retrieving the senior meals with no gloves

when she returns safely
I say, *Sorry, sorry.* She says, *Sorry, sorry*
we wash hands

I hide my tears
twenty-three years together
we have never felt more uncertain

we make handwritten wills
extra copies of our dnr/domestic partnership papers
turn off news listen to the country station

watch the marchers from our bedroom window
kiss hug cry
wash hands again again—

MAGNIFICENT FLOWER

I lived five decades with you
my umber-brown boy glowing
warm against my chest.

Suddenly I am without you,
magnificent flower of my womb.
What name do you call me now son?

The wind will come for these words
the only thing you will have left behind
is your breath written on tree bark.

LEARNING TO WALK: THE FIRST YEAR AFTER HIS DEATH

For Ceni

days and months of not eating not
sleeping and she leaving on the lights at
night cooking feeding insulin reminders
turning down covers arranging
rearranging flowers ice packs heating pads

weeks and weeks make the bed help me in
offering the very end of a smile
waking with my soul half gone
burning the body to its edge

guilt sitting crossed leg
sippin champagne like she was an invited guest
blame remorse fear shame
blood in swollen right eye
sight blurred

painkillers heart monitor ct scan
pacemaker
chiropractor acupuncture acupressure
reiki cbd oil psychologist two hundred
per session
insurance won't cover

before that night
there was our engagement
my body lifted and went to venus
then came wedding planning
cake tasting dress making fabric choices
music/champagne selection
white blush France Spain Long Island

then he's not
not responding
fear of waking answering the phone
watching tv going outside
on the subway airplanes crowded streets

fear of going to sleep dreams nightmares
thinking about dying living
fear of eating sleeping dreaming fucking
kissing

finally she said
how long
babe

and I said softly in the voice of a haiku

my biggest fear is
that you will leave me because
I am sad, I said

my love, if you think that
you should leave me because I'm
not doing my job, she said
pinkie swear you will try to walk
she makes me swear over and over again

now let's walk!

FARE LEFT UNPAID

For Mom at twenty-two

Count the splinters on her legs
the bruises on her elbows
count the dollar bills
tossed coins
her green plastic change purse
the rhinestone comb from her hair
broken gold chain
count the cracked window
and taxi fare unpaid
count his curses
her screams
her house keys left behind
picture of her newborn baby boy soaked in the mud
count the scratches on his face
and bite mark on his forearm
count his rageful growl
his fingers a thousand red fire ants
blood falling from her lips
and she never told how she held her tears
or about her broken tooth
or how she jumped out of the moving taxi
or the scratchy bushes where she hid
she never told
how his breath smelled like poison
or how she feared that nasty scent would never leave
his eyes like a raging animal's
left her blind
count the teeth marks
and the blows
his crazy wild man laughter
his fare left unpaid

JEWELS

I tried to write my mother's ache
her terror her pulse her sight
thirteen small garnets jewels for each eye   look!

STILL MARCHING

oh God George Floyd damn
brother son father
ancestors say call and we always there

DaunteWrightMarvinScottRayshardBooksTonyMcDade
ElijahMcClainJavierAmblerJaylandWalker

ah curse an cry up ah storm
stupes when de hot pot burn meh hand
stupes when de tears shine meh eye

is months now ah angry
yuh tink after all this time I'd git used to
scratching this wicked plot of world

help meh mother
you know meh well
send meh back to myself

ah angry storm just hit meh yard
smashed clay pots tigerlilies
and fresh green peas

tomatoes nearly ripe but dem nah sweet
meh Easter dress press in de hall closet
de church door lock no way to pray

I don't do marches anymore
meh lef foot duz hurt meh

CLINTON HILL, BROOKLYN

First of June twenty twenty-two
we sat on the tiny balcony
munching homemade guacamole

salt free chips, heavy onions, loads of pepper
Ceni made the sangria extra sour
with mango slices & fresh limes
we played Beyoncé *Love on Top*
sang loud danced slow
it's been a long time since our arms felt so full

THE LIMITLESS HEART

Slow dancing

I refuse one more day of mourning
come lover
fill my mouth with a thousand kisses
woman there is so much left to do
I fear us getting old feeding on all this loss
give me some sun yellow tulips
and a slow dance for all the loving
all the lovers I ever held

Yes

yes, I was married
yes, she was married too
yes, she kissed me first
yes, I kissed her back
yes, our spirits flew
yes, she smelled like apple blossoms
yes, earth said glory
yes, I held my breath
yes, we cried yes, yes
yes, she sang out loud
yes, she called me daddy
yes, the moon raised a brow
yes, the ocean came to see
yes, I heard the fierce beating of my heart
yes, there were hidden poems
yes, that was fucked up
yes, we could not stop
yes, I could not let go
yes, it went on for years
yes, someone got hurt
yes, I got no alimony
yes, we had regret
yes, I should be filled with shame
yes, I'd do it all again

Finally, Elma

Notes on love

Finally, you have your mother's face
her body round and doughy
you own it you've worked very hard for it

you hear yourself saying words like surely and oh good Lord
and pass me not oh gentle savior
and dat man is a scamp

and about the man she loved after my father
she says with pride look at me eh
I choose a good man

Darnel so unassuming you'd never know he was a big doctor
people see he there small and black black
huh he had plenty power
work hard for all ah it too

on my twenty-first birthday she said
girl stop picking them people who have big potential
and nothing to follow it up with
when you making chiren man must have de right ingredients

that one you love last year is a thief and a scoundrel
and de one now is a Venus fly trap
wait lil bit nah daughter
take time wa yuh rushing so for

and back then I thought
she always butting in
nobody ask she no questions
but she got answers

and just last night I heard my mother's mouth say
to my grandson
Dave I don't like that girl
she lil bit too loud n pushy

every girl who like you
you don't have to like honey
take your time son
why yuh rushing so

an I heard Elma mouth
an ai eh even feel shame self
not bad nothing but big big pride

Birthday Party for Aunt V at 100

She takes my hand I kiss her cheek
My dear niece ai live a good life
three girls all brown n pretty
wid no damn man to bother me

dis virus ain't bout no flu
yuh smart Cherry yuh know
some man make it in China
stupid corolla virus

dat ugly man on Pennsylvania Avenue
pay plenty for it
yuh know he evil
like de devil

huh I really doh care what dey do now
all I know ai eh want to lose meh deposit money
for meh birthday party
de better hurry an finish wid this damn corolla
ai been waiting to dance all year

my family got to hug and kiss me
pet me up much much
I deserve it being the jewel
oldest in de family I is queen

when my time come
I want to sleep and never wake
doh bring no set ah cryin' here neither
all'yuh had me long enuf

yuh goin' to see to dat eh darlin'
yes
yuh love meh ai love you
I brush her hair   she takes my hand

Recipe to Write a Life

Count sunflowers on the first day they arrive
hold family recipes in head
hire a cleaning service send out wash

cinnamon-ginger tea each morning
hold in your body a singing like running water
house everything at your pen's tip
pray to start each day

hear your father's voice
know that elegant song anywhere
carry with pride that birth certificate
that says illegitimate

eight and your arms outstretched
wide like grandma's back bedroom window
open for rain goldfinches
and twin brother to return

write a poem to sea
it's always aqua-blue
near cousin Eutrice house

in red bean garlic soup
add basmati rice and pig tails
wait for sweet boy
to cuddle your face

his kisses flying high
over shoulder and gaze
babe I still have that mama face
what shall I do with it

IN THE SEVENTH DECADE

I'm looking fly in that bright mango dress
that fly-ass off the shoulder head-turner
I be seventy
still I count all the ways I don't feel pretty or useful anymore
it is poem-a-day month I count the hours flying by with no poems
pretty soon it will be midnight and not one line
To distract myself I stack dishes in the dishwasher teacups lined up in colorful rows
I go in search of stubby gray chin hairs who refuse to be evicted
I pause
inhale garlic and olive oil in the fresh kale salad
a faithful pot of brown rice still on the stove
The last year tweezers and black hair dye have become my best friends
Lord count the tweezers I lost this week alone
Heavy cups of black coffee bring me life
Forgive me as I count the days my brain sat unused
days when I walked into a room only to forget why I was there
I need more memorizing and note-taking
but I still chipper
got my cranberry-red lipstick always on the ready

SHE LED ME

I came to Ntozake's class
in search of poems

She sent me for coffee
had me make phone calls
write the class assignment
on the blackboard
collect fees at the door

She said
the dancer goes to the barre every day
a poet must go to their writing table you must write
write your ass off every day
every day

It was Ntozake
who led me to Cheryl Clarke
to *Living as a Lesbian*
skin of that summer well spent
it was Cheryl Clarke who said
stop asking questions
about whose voice is this or that
who is saying what
just write woman write
think of yourself as a medium through which work flows

Cheryl led me to Audre Lorde
after I said Audre invited me to her writing class
and I'm scared to go
she said girl go to that class and show out
I did and began using words as weapons

then it was June Jordan
her voice a red chiffon robe left on the floor

and Kimiko Hahn and her meandering road to zuihitsu
and Alexis Pauline Gumbs and her *Revolutionary Mothering*
and Lucille Clifton that landscape of a good woman
hands on hips
showing us again what we came here to do

who guided me to Nikky Finney   Nikky I found that big old bimbo gal
you warned me of
that big-ass mouth waiting in my notebook
both grandmothers watching

since then I have not wanted to do anything else
but write and hold that woman that I love
you told me I would love myself too Nikky

de Trini backwater poems came
the white sage and cayenne pepper I poured into my pen grew and grew
like that wreck of a sweet mouth I built for me
fine as it could be

Acknowledgments

Grateful acknowledgment is made to the following publishers for permission to reprint poems from the following titles:

Raw Air
Fly By Night Press, 1997
In Association With A Gathering of The Tribes
Steve Cannon

Night When Moon Follows
Long Shot Publications, 2000
Danny Shot

Convincing The Body
Vintage Entity Press, 2005
Steven G. Fullwood

Arrival
TriQuarterly Books/Northwestern University Press, 2017
Parneshia Jones

Mama Phife Represents
Haymarket Books/BreakBeat Poets Series 2021
Maya Marshall

We Are Not Wearing Helmets
TriQuarterly Books/ Northwestern University Press, 2022
Parneshia Jones

Sincerest gratitude is made to the editors of the following journals and magazines where some of these poems in varying versions first appeared: *Aloud: Voices from the Nuyorican Poets Café*, Chelsea, #64, Jacob's Pillow Dance Festival, The Joyce Theatre New York City, EVIDENCE: A Dance Company, *Bullets and Butterflies: Queer Spoken Word Poetry, Revolutionary Mothering: Love On the Front Lines, The Mom Egg Review, Small Axe Press,* and *Killens Review of Arts & Letters.*

A huge shout out to my poetry peeps: Yesenia Montilla, Elma's Heart Circle, aracelis girmay, Sabrina Hayeem-Ladani, and my entire family at Haymarket Books, including Nisha Bolsey, who I thank for her keen eye and generous spirit. Special thanks to Jacqueline Johnson, Kevin Powell, Randall Horton, Nancy Mercado, Mahogany L. Browne, Walt Taylor, Kate Quarfordt for the cover artwork, and Dominique Sindayiganza for the author photo.

And to: Maya Marshall, Mom, Desciana Swinger, Donna Lee Weber, Deisha Head Taylor.

And to Malik Izaak Taylor: it all started with you...
We made a home of words; I still live there.

About the Author

Photo by Dominique Sindayiganza

Cheryl Boyce-Taylor is a poet and teaching artist. She earned an MFA from Stonecoast at the University of Southern Maine and an MSW from Fordham University. She is the author of five previous collections of poetry—*Raw Air* (1997), *Night When Moon Follows* (2000), *Convincing the Body* (2005), *Arrival* (2017), and *We Are Not Wearing Helments* (2022)—and a memoir and poetic tribute to her son, *Mama Phife Represents*. *Mama Phife Represents* won Publishing Triangle's Audre Lorde Award for Lesbian Poetry and was listed as one of New York Public Library's Best Books of 2021.

A VONA fellow, Boyce-Taylor is the founder and curator of Calypso Muse and the Glitter Pomegranate Performance Series. Her poetry has been commissioned by the The Joyce Theater and the National Endowment for the Arts for Ronald K. Brown's EVIDENCE, A Dance Company. She has led numerous poetry workshops for Cave Canem, the New York Public Library, Urban Word NYC, and Poets House, among others. Her life papers and portfolio are stored at the Schomburg Center for Research in Black Culture in New York City. She lives in Brooklyn.

About Haymarket Books

Haymarket Books is a radical, independent, nonprofit book publisher based in Chicago. Our mission is to publish books that contribute to struggles for social and economic justice. We strive to make our books a vibrant and organic part of social movements and the education and development of a critical, engaged, and internationalist Left.

We take inspiration and courage from our namesakes, the Haymarket Martyrs, who gave their lives fighting for a better world. Their 1886 struggle for the eight-hour day—which gave us May Day, the international workers' holiday—reminds workers around the world that ordinary people can organize and struggle for their own liberation. These struggles—against oppression, exploitation, environmental devastation, and war—continue today across the globe.

Since our founding in 2001, Haymarket has published more than nine hundred titles. Radically independent, we seek to drive a wedge into the risk-averse world of corporate book publishing. Our authors include Angela Y. Davis, Arundhati Roy, Keeanga-Yamahtta Taylor, Eve L. Ewing, aja monet, Mariame Kaba, Naomi Klein, Rebecca Solnit, Olúfémi O. Táíwò, Mohammed El-Kurd, José Olivarez, Noam Chomsky, Winona LaDuke, Robyn Maynard, Leanne Betasamosake Simpson, Howard Zinn, Mike Davis, Marc Lamont Hill, Dave Zirin, Astra Taylor, and Amy Goodman, among many other leading writers of our time. We are also the trade publishers of the acclaimed Historical Materialism Book Series.

Haymarket also manages a vibrant community organizing and event space in Chicago, Haymarket House, the popular Haymarket Books Live event series and podcast, and the annual Socialism Conference.

Also Available from Haymarket Books

All the Blood Involved in Love, Maya Marshall

Black Queer Hoe, Britteney Black Rose Kapri

The BreakBeat Poets Vol. 2: Black Girl Magic, ed. by Mahogany L. Browne, Idrissa Simmonds, and Jamila Woods

Build Yourself a Boat, Camonghne Felix

Can I Kick It?, Idris Goodwin

Citizen Illegal, José Olivarez

I Remember Death by Its Proximity to What I Love, Mahogany L. Browne

Lineage of Rain, Janel Pineda

Mama Phife Represents, Cheryl Boyce-Taylor

Milagro, Penelope Allegria

The Patron Saint of Making Curfew, Tim Stafford

Rifqa, Mohammed El-Kurd

Super Sad Black Girl, Diamond Sharp

There Are Trans People Here, H. Melt

Too Much Midnight, Krista Franklin

Printed in the USA
CPSIA information can be obtained
at www.ICGtesting.com
JSHW081030290823
47455JS00001B/1